Notes
70% of learning comes from taking notes.

Notes
70% of learning comes from taking notes.

Check List
100% of learning is by doing

- Activity 1 (page 39)
- Activity 2 (page 45)
- Activity 3 (page 51)
- Activity 4 (page 63)
- Activity 5 (page 71)
- Activity 6 (page 78)
- Activity 7 (page 89)
- Activity 8 (page 99)
- Activity 9 (page 104)
- Activity 10 (page 109)
- Activity 11 (page 115)
- Activity 12 (page 123)

Can You Hear Me Now?

Raise your standards and stop making excuses!

By Steven Walker

831 DESIGNS UK

831 Designs is part of Forever Family Forever Free group of Companies whose address can be found at ForeverFamilyForeverFree.com.

First published in the United Kingdom by Amazon

Copyright © 2017 by Steven Walker.
All rights reserved.

No part of these pages, either text or image may be used for any purpose other than personal use. Therefore, reproduction, modification, storage in a retrieval system or retransmission, in any form or by any means, electronic, mechanical or otherwise, for reasons other than personal use, is strictly prohibited without prior written permission.

    First published 2017
    831 Designs
    London. UK
    www.831Designs.com

Book: Can You Hear Me Now?
Steven Walker. -- 1st ed.
**ISBN-13:
978-1976220685**

**ISBN-10:
1976220688**

Foreword

I don't know about you but I believe that human nature is to reward effort. I'm not talking about effort where a person goes one time and doesn't get what they want and gives up. I'm talking about an in your face daily action to get the attention of another. I'm talking about a willingness to see something through to its logical conclusion. I'm talking about an uncommon resilience to exchange value with another and help them advance their ball down the field toward a dominant focus. This is the kind of effort Steven Walker gives. He makes sure "you can hear him now." He makes sure, through a variety of messages, special gifts, advocacy, and a likable personality that he gets and keeps your attention. He's a pro at promoting and this is exactly what you want from a person who is helping you promote your goods and services to the world.

The greatest challenge of the small business owner who wants so desperately to become big is not capital. It's not talent. It's not the product. It's not being known by enough people.

Steven pushes hard in this book to help you "become known." The world-famous means well known, renown, and celebrated. It means that more people know you than you know them. It means that your work is inspiring to others and you are creating value that the world is rewarding in the form of love, money, recognition, and referrals.

"Can you hear me now" is a book about the real effort it takes to be heard in a NOISY and DISTRACTED world. It's a book by a person who worked like a pro

Can You Hear Me Now?

to get my attention and got in the boat with me until he got what he wanted and that's this forward.

I reward effort. You're going to be rewarded by digging into this work and building the capacity you really need to get noticed every single day.

Coach Micheal Burt
The Super Coach
Founder of Monster Producer
Author of "Everybody Needs a Coach in Life

A Special Thank you

In this book, I will mention so many people that have and continue to inspire me and impact me. The one person who has stuck by my side longer than anyone else?... Is Cassie Jo Walker. My beautiful wife, thank you for seeing something in me that most did not, and most of all thank you for never leaving me. You must have seen things in me that I never knew I had because you always pushed me in the right direction. I am convinced you are the woman of Proverbs 31. That is the one I always wished and prayed for. You are a better mother to our kids than I ever dreamed was possible. You help me in any way you can, and you don't give me too hard of a time. You are always willing to suck it up and do the next right thing. We both know this has been a bumpy ride. I predict the future will be very bright if we have each other. I know I don't speak my feelings to you enough, but what better way to share how much you mean to me than in words, in the front of my first book.

If it was not for you I would not be the 3 of my favourite things in this world. A Husband, a Father, and a Businessman. I would like to use an analogy that I know you will appreciate. In fishing, there's a rod and a reel. Not necessarily a need but I never go without mine. I have a complex reel and a sturdy rod. On the reel there is line and it runs through the eyes of the rod and then attached to a hook and some bait. Let me tell you this, I can have the perfect rod and reel Set.

Can You Hear Me Now?

I can have the perfect hooks and bait. I can even be in a Place where monster fish are but, you know without some good tough line to tie it all together with it's all worthless. Cassie, you are the line that helped me tie all the different parts of my life together.

I Reel-y Do Love You.

Can you hear me now Sweetheart?

Contents

1	Who Can Hear Me Now?	15
2	Why I Feel the Need to Be Heard	41
3	How I Did It	47
4	Persistence/ Do What You Say	53
5	Believe in Yourself	65
6	Take Action	73
7	Don't Quit Until the Bell Rings	79
8	Care About People	91
9	Be Willing to Give	101
10	Don't Tolerate Being Unheard	115
11	Be Willing to Hear NO	111
12	Having the Right Attitude	117
	Final Chapter How I Can Help You?	125
	About the Author	131
	Thank You	133
	Dedication	143

Can You Hear Me Now?

"YOU DON'T HAVE TO BE GREAT TO START, BUT YOU HAVE TO START TO BE GREAT"

Zig Ziglar

CHAPTER ONE

Who Can Hear Me Now?

I would like to start my book by telling you the different people that I've been able to get the attention of. The reason I'm doing this is not to brag, but to lend credibility to my story. I could get these people's attention with the limited skills and resources in less than a year's time. I believe that I can help anyone do the same things that I have done. For those people that are willing to learn and put what I say into practice, this could really change your business or even your life, like I was able to do. The people that I am mentioning here in this book are people that I did not know or have links to prior to this new strategy. I feel like it's very important to mention that none of these people would know who I am if I had not practiced persistence and gift giving. Knowing these people now has changed my life and my business in a huge way. These people are considered friends and mentors to me. Some of them are even customers. I am writing this book because I have a passion to help more people be heard period, I want to share the principles and concepts that I have been using to get these people's attention. If I can do it with my limited amount of skills and resources, I know I can help anyone from the very beginning of your business or once they are fully established. I can get you more attention for your business.

Who Can Hear Me Now?

Can You Hear Me Now?

JJ Jackintelle

I heard JJ Jackintelle speak at the 10xgrowthcon and the things he said about culture, not only for his business but for his family, changed the way I do things in both of those areas of my life. I reached out to J.J. Several times asking him for his address and not getting any response from him. I then found a great photo of him and his wife, I had it designed onto a Ten Four Battery Pack. I then did a live video which I tagged him. He got on there and didn't say anything. I told him I will find you buddy and you will get this gift I had made for you! I messaged him afterward and he didn't respond one bit. Looking back at that moment I found it was frustrating. I had a customized gift for him but not an address. A friend reached out and gave me an address that he believed was J.J.'s. I sent J.J. a message and said is this it? He responded he said yes. I was finally able to send him my gift along with a personal thank you card! He then did an Instagram Post thanking me for my gift! Since then he has trusted the Battery Packs for his kids who are both away at college. He bought one for each of them. His new Business Car saver is

Who Can Hear Me Now?

now a Customer of ours and we couldn't be happier about working with such a great company.
Best Quotes
"Very cool gift from Steven Walker at Walker Promotes. Thank you... the way to one's heart is give them "juice" to run their life. awesome charger!! Will be checking out your other products."

Who Can Hear Me Now?

Micheal Burt

I came across Super Coach Micheal Burt one day while I was watching Brad Lea's videos on YouTube. Something about this Coach really caught my attention. The way he talks makes him a person of interest to me. He doesn't cuss or say stupid things. He carries himself in a very professional way. I had the honour of meeting Coach at the 10xgrowthcon in the lobby of the Diplomat. He was very polite and very interested in me and how I was Branding myself. I had some huge headphones around my neck and a big-name tag on my jacket that had Walker Promotes on it. He was very complimentary and I really appreciated that. After the conference, I sent him a thank you card but never heard anything back. This guy Coaches Monster Producers so his time is very laser focused and it is tough to get his attention. I didn't give up. I continued to watch his free content on YouTube and Facebook. The more I did this the more I liked him. Finally, I had a Ten Four Battery pack made with the cover of his newest book on it. "Everybody

Can You Hear Me Now?

Needs a Coach in Life" I then wrote another card telling Coach how much I appreciate him and what he does daily. I sent the package out. For some reason Coach didn't get it right away so I had to be very persistent to ensure that it arrived. It took about a month but it was well worth the wait. He appreciated the gift very much and I believe we will be doing business together very soon. I am so grateful to him for writing the foreword for this book.
Best Quotes
" Steven Walker this is Coach Burt. I want to say a big shout out, big guy. Thank you for the goods. They have arrived. Appreciate your brother, it means a lot to me."

Who Can hear me now?

Rondi Lambeth

I first Saw Rondi On Brad Lea's Live Video. Rondi has the only Paid upon Performance Credit Repair Company "Fortress Credit Pro." I like him instantly and added him as a friend on FB. I watched his videos daily about how I too could fix my credit and ultimately live better. I got so much value from his videos I decided that I wanted to thank him. I went on his FB and found a photo of him and his Wife Michelle. I created it on a Ten Four Battery pack and sent it to him along with my personal Handwritten thank you card, and shortly after he received it he did a great FB live video showing his appreciation. A month or so after the video he bought some Fortress Credit Pro Polo shirts from me for his staff. I am proud to now call his company a customer. In July I made a trip to go and visit him, and I could spend a whole 10 hours with Rondi and his amazing Wife Michelle. I ate dinner with them and had excellent conversations. I could discuss in detail what I'm passionate about and ask Rondi questions about my

Can You Hear Me Now?

business and how I should tweak things to make it better. I left their house that night not only having them as customers but as friends. I'm confident that I'll never forget Rondi and his wife and I won't ever let them forget me.

Best Quotes
" This is a great idea. I had no idea I was getting this. There is some cool stuff in here.... (reads handwritten thank you card out loud). That's freaking awesome dude, that's awesome! Now let's see what's inside. This is a great idea. You got a product log book. Those are some cool headphones, I could send some of these to my credit repair clients, you can send them as gifts. This is a great idea what you are doing here. I mean versus sending me an email. This costs a lot more than sending an email but this is a lot more powerful. We are going to get some of those (video brochures), so that might have paid for this gift. What do you think this is? External battery pack, this is so cool. Check this out. This is a little charger and here you can charge multiple things. My wife is going to love this, I love it! Now check this what is cool about it. Look how cool that is. That was my wedding day with my wife. I guess he got it off Facebook. Isn't that sweet! Now my phone will never die during a Facebook live because I will make sure I always have this with me all the time. Thank you, Steven! If you guys want cool stuff like this for you or your customers get in touch with Walker Promotes.

Who Can hear me now?

" If you guys need any promotional products, shirts, battery packs for your phones that I use on a regular basis, pens, anything that has your logo on, Steven Walker of Walker Promotes is the guy you need to see about getting that stuff fixed."

Who Can hear me now?

Roddy Chong

I first heard about Roddy Chong at the 10xgrowthcon. He is an excellent Violin Player but not only that he has an amazing success story. I decided after the Conference I wanted to get his attention, so I found a photo on Google of Roddy rocking on the violin and put it on our Ten Four Battery Pack. I then did a live video where I tagged Roddy, showed the Battery Pack that I planned to send him. Roddy then shared the FB Live Video. Don't take my word for it! You can go to @RoddyChong on Fb and find the post!
He Said, *"Dude Got My Attention"*

Can You Hear Me Now?

John Hamlin

I met John Hamlin at the 10xgrowthcon. We had a nice conversation. The thing that stuck out to me the most about John is that his mentor told him the same that my mentor told me. "They put their pants on the same way that I do". He said this to encourage me and it was very effective. After the conference, I felt the need to reach out and thank John so found a photo on John's FB page of Grant Cardone and John on his Private Jet. I had a Ten Four Battery pack with this photo on it and had it sent to my house. I then took one of my thank you cards with my logo on it and wrote a note in it thanking him for his time at the conference. I shipped it out and just a few days later I received a call from John and he was saying thank you for the gift. Shortly after that, I could get an order from John's Company Hamlin and Associates. I am proud to call them a customer today.

Best Quotes
"Hey man, thank you so much for sending me this. Give me a call today."

Who Can hear me now?

Matt Manero

You can read the story of how we met in chapter 7
Best Quotes
" I do see gifts as valuable in an opportunity to get attention."

"Thanks for the great gifts Steven Walker. These are awesome promo gifts."

Can You Hear Me Now?

Danelle Delgado

You can read the story of how we met in chapter 5 Best Quotes
"Steven Walker I used your charger today. Thank you!"

"Thank you, Steve Walker, for making our amazing shirts. Walker Promotes, he's amazing."

"Hey Steve Walker I shared you last Friday night and on the live video I did last week from Hawaii I did with my charger. I love it. Thank you so much! I needed it. It saved me in Hawaii."

This man just drove 9 hours to come take us to coffee (after our FB Live last night)!!
#winning #The Exception

Who Can hear me now?
Brad Lea

You can read the story of how we met in chapter 9 Best Quotes
" Steven Walker you da man. Sending me this type of stuff is awesome but it is also a lesson. He took money out of his own pocket took his own time, got them customized sent them out here all of that costs money all of that takes time and now he's got my attention."

" We are probably going to put in order into Walker Promotes just simply because he is going above and beyond."

" In order to get that attention and get somebody to notice you sometimes you got to make an investment, sometimes you got to go outside the box put a little money where your mouth is and knock it out." "If you guys need shirts, Steven Walker, the one incessantly telling you I have shirts, is the one you would get your shirts from. Also, he's got these little battery packs that are just badass. Those things are helpful son of guns. By the way Walker I will be going down on the 19th to hang out on the shark tank

Can You Hear Me Now?

set so I will personally deliver Mr, Daymond John's battery pack that you made for him and I'll let him know you sent it to him."

"I've got some new shirts coming in from Steven Walker who sold me some goods."

"There's Steven Walker. Man, that guy's like fricking Jesus. He's everywhere."

"Take Steven Walker. I'm sure he's watching. The guy will bother you till no end. He'll call you 700 times with his headphones on asking if you want battery packs or any kind of promotional material which by the way I buy promotional material from Steven Walker. If you need promotional material call, Steven Walker, he's a good hard-working dude."

"How do you get attention in sales? A guy named Steven Walker unsolicited sent me these awesome customized battery packs out of the blue. This guy calls me, tries to get my attention, tries to get me to buy his products and of course, I don't necessarily buy and what does he do? He sends me some stuff."

"I want to do 2 things. 1 Thank this guy, Steven Walker you da man. Sending me this type of stuff is awesome but it is also a lesson. He took money out of his own pocket took his own time, got them customized sent them out here all that costs money all of that takes time and now he's got my attention. I'm starting to see some of the things he has where out of 100 people a day hit me up to buy my swag from. My hats, t-shirts all kinds of things and now

Who Can hear me now?

because this guy is listening to the content we are putting out and using his brain and getting attention and going above and beyond the norm, he's got my attention. And two guess what we are probably going to put in order into Walker Promotes just simply because he is going above and beyond. He is applying some of the information, he's learning and taking a step in the right direction at least to get my business very similarly to a lot of people that I know. To get that attention and get somebody to notice you sometimes you got to make an investment, sometimes you got to go outside the box put a little money where your mouth is and knock it out."

Who Can hear me now?

Elena Cardone

Elena Cardone is a remarkable woman. She is also married to Grant Cardone. I had been working to get Grant's attention with very little luck, my wife and I decided to send Elena some gifts. We sent her some 10xQueen tank tops and a Battery Pack with a photo of her holding her favourite Pistol! She was so appreciative of these gifts and even gave us shout outs on Their Fb Live **The G&E Show** where she even showed some of the products we sent!
Best Quotes
" The battery packs are really awesome. They have really proved to be a lifesaver on more than one occasion. Really a great product."

Who Can hear me now?

Grant Cardone

As I recall all the people I have mentioned in this book, I am reminded that if it was not for Grant Cardone, I would not know about many of these people. It all started with him. I decided about a year prior to writing this book that I wanted to do business with GC and that I would do WHATEVER it takes to achieve that. It has been quite a journey. I have spent countless hours studying and learning from this man and so many of his business partners and friends. I have been a guest on his show on a couple different occasions via the phone. He has given me multiple shout outs on his FB and Instagram. I have sent him several gifts that I thought he would find extremely useful in his business and travels, with his logo on them. He is currently using the Battery Pack every day that we sent him. Nobody understands the importance of getting attention quite like GC does. He is in many different areas of business and he is doing very well in each area. You can't get on social media without seeing him, and he will be in your inbox every day. He gets attention! He is the Best Salesman of all time. Period. I could make it to

Can You Hear Me Now?

his 10xgrowthcon event in 2017. I had two encounters with the man himself. The first time I had an opportunity at the conference was while a speaker was performing. I was out in the lobby and not many people were out there. Grant walked by quickly and I saw the 10xgrowthcon Battery pack that I had sent him. This was my chance. I loudly but Gently said Grant how do you like the charger? He stepped towards me, he looked directly into my eyes, put out his hand to shake mine, and said thank you. The second encounter was so unreal. It was recorded live or I would not have believed that it happened. Grant opened it up for Q&A on the last day and I was the first one to literally run up to the front of the stage and I asked him two questions.

How Important Is It to Get Attention in Sales?
Do I have yours?
The way he answered these questions were a huge lesson and I want this to stick with you. He said, "It is everything, and yes you do." Grant, I know at some point you will read this book, and I hope you will finally realize all the work that I have done to connect with you and to do business with you. The great part about having this huge goal, using all my persistence and more to create a relationship, and business deal with you, is that it has helped me learn so much about myself, and gain so much more connections and business ventures. I have been able to do business with lots of your friends and partners. I have gained tons of confidence. I am learning more about Business and Sales each day, and I have learned a whole new concept for me to expand upon which is

Who Can hear me now?

the Gift Giving. A big thank you to you is in order, but words can't express my gratitude.
Mr. Cardone.
My question to you is

"Can You Hear Me Now?"

A gift opens the way and ushers the giver into the presence of the great.
Proverbs 18:16

Action Steps

1) Make a list of all the big players in your industry.

a)

b)

c)

d)

e)

2) How having them as customers / clients could change your business.

a)

b)

c)

d)

e)

CHAPTER TWO

Why I feel the need to be heard.

I would like to tell you a little bit of why I am the way that I am. I want to tell you why I will not tolerate being unheard. This all started at a very young age, I lived with my mom from the time I was born until I was about 13 years old. She was mentally and physically abusive to me. As a child, I had no voice. She would say things like, "Children are supposed to be seen and not heard." I really internalized that. Then at the age of 13, I was sent to go live with my father. I remember really wanting his attention, but he was involved in a brand-new marriage to my stepmom today. It just seemed like, from a kid's perspective, that I didn't really have a place there. I remember always wanting to be heard. I was reminded of this a while back and I would write him letters and I would put them in his boots so that when he woke up in the morning, he would have to hear what I had to say. I am not sure

Can You Hear Me Now?

why I felt that but I just remember that, and it stuck in my mind. It didn't work out at my dad's house, with him and my stepmom. I was then placed into foster care till age 13. For those of you who don't know, as a foster child, it is a lonely feeling. I didn't have any family involved. I didn't feel like I had anybody that I could talk to. I always remember just feeling like I didn't have a voice at all. I was in foster care until I graduated high school. Then when I graduated high school, I went to college, and then I felt the need to be heard and to be known. I felt the need to act out so that people would notice me and so that people would like me. I mean, that's really what it boiled down to, I wanted people to like me, but for them to like me, they would have to hear me. They would have to know who I was. They would have to be able to relate to me and what I've been through. I started hanging out with the wrong people solely because they were the ones that would pay attention to me. I ended up going to prison for possession of Marijuana, I was young and stupid and lacking

Why I feel the need to be heard.

connection. This was another situation in my life where I had no voice. It didn't matter what my

thoughts and opinions were. I was told when I could eat when I needed to go to sleep when I had to go to bed, all of that. So, this lifelong obsession of being heard must lead me to this incredible tool in business. This whole life of mine, I have felt like I didn't have a voice.

Action Steps

1) Think of the biggest most negative things that have affected you in the past.

2) How have these negative challenges positivity influenced you and your life now that you can see the bigger picture?

a)

b)

c)

d)

e)

CHAPTER THREE

How I did it.

Prior to writing this book, I started on my personal development journey. The biggest, greatest thing that I came across, that meant the most to me, that has made the biggest difference in my life is that I am worth something. I do have self-worth. I do have a voice. I do have opinions and thoughts that can help people. I have not only a responsibility but an obligation and a duty to make sure that my voice is heard. That is what fuels this appetite, this that seems is an insatiable appetite to be heard. I always felt like nobody was listening to me. That is why I am writing this book. That is why I feel like I'm more successful now, because I have raised my standards, dropped my excuses, and I will not tolerate being unheard. Since I started implementing being persistent and gifting into my business and my life, I have noticed a lot of changes. I have been able to create a lot more connections and create a lot more

Can You Hear Me Now?

business across the world. My voice is being heard. You are starting to respond to my messages, you are not only hearing me and seeing me, but you are starting to know me. You are starting to like me and you are starting to support me. I have been able to do all of this. I have been able to get these people's attention, then go on to do business with some of these multi-millionaires with very little resources. As I will mention in detail, later, I spent about $2,000 on this whole idea of gifting.

If a guy like me at the position that I am in right now can get these people's attention, think how much more I can do to help you with your business. If I can do business with them, I must have found something that really sets me apart from the crowd. Three things I have really been practicing and implementing is persistence, attitude, and gifting. I do what I say, and I believe in what I am doing so much so that I don't take no for an answer. It keeps me going. I don't ever stop, but then I have people that continue to ignore me. I believe that I can help their business. I believe that I can help

How I did it.

them get more attention for their brand, but a lot of these multi-millionaires, are looking at me as somebody that doesn't have anything figured out, or anything to offer because I don't have millions yet. Sometimes it can be hard to convince them that they need to send gifts or that they need to get more attention for themselves. I have simple questions that I ask them. Are any of your prospects ignoring you? Are they all answering your phone calls? Are they all answering your emails? Many would say that somebody in their life is ignoring them. What I have done in this moment when I am being ignored, I will take a little bit of money out of my pocket, time and effort to create it, and I will get a gift that's personal to the person that is ignoring me. I will send it to them. Then almost immediately the person will reach back out to me and say, "Hey, I've just been busy. Yadda, yadda, yadda." Then, BOOM. "Thank you for the gift. Now, what do you have in mind? How can I help you?" Then that gift opens the doors to allow more opportunities.

Action Steps

1) Visit Walkerpromotes.com

2) Make a list of your 5 favourite products for ideas.

    a)
    b)
    c)
    d)
    e)

3) Make a list of who you could send them to.

    a)
    b)
    c)
    d)
    e)

CHAPTER FOUR

Persistence / Do what you Say

A big part of being persistent is doing exactly what you say you're going to do. I find today that so many people are loose with their words. They'll say that they'll be somewhere, or they'll say that they'll call someone or just say that they're going to do something and they do not do it. It seems to be quite all right to not do what you say you're going to do. People's/societies standards have slipped.

There are people that will say those things, and they have the best intentions of following through and doing what they say, but when it comes time for them to do it, they just simply don't. Then they will have excuses, they will have all these great reasons for why they're not doing what they say. I feel it's just complete nonsense to not do what you say you're going to do.

It's very easy to not say something unless you know for a fact that you can do it. The biggest part of being

Can You Hear Me Now?

persistent for me is just doing what you say you're going to do. Raise your standards and stop making excuses!

This goes for all areas of your life. If you say you're going to lose weight, then you need to do the things that are necessary to do that. If you say you're going to spend more time with your kids, then you need to do that. You need to take the time, you need to set the time aside and follow through with what you say you're going to do.

Not doing what you say you're going to do, can cause lots of problems. One of the biggest problems it causes is if you say you're going to do something and you don't, then you'll stop believing in yourself. You will stop believing in what it is that you can do and what it is that you can accomplish.

So, for example, if I say, "I'm going to lose 100 pounds" and I get going and I get started on a good diet and an exercise plan and I go about that for a month or two and then I quit, deep down inside I'm telling myself that I can't lose that weight. When I don't follow through with that, then I'm just setting

Persistence / Do what you Say

myself up for failure in the future. So, in the future, I won't be willing to try certain things because I will remember that time when I said, "I'm going to lose weight" and then I didn't follow through. I couldn't do that. Raise your standards and stop making excuses!

It is also very important in business to do what you say when you said you would do it. If you tell someone you're going to call them at 2:00, you need to do that. You need to have the respect for them, but also for yourself. Don't waste your time. If you've got an appointment at 2:00, make sure that you're not late. I would even be a little bit early. I would err on the side of caution and turn 10-15 minutes early. It is said, if you are ten minutes early you are on time if you are on time you are late and if you are late, it is unacceptable.

When you're dealing with big hitters, guru's in the business world, multi-millionaires etc. the types of people that I've been going after, the people that I've been working hard to get the attention of, I feel it's

Can You Hear Me Now?

even more important to do what you say. When you say you're going to do it, because the masses are not doing what they say, they are doing a lot of talking, they are saying a lot of good stuff, but the highly successful people aren't just believing everything you say. They're waiting to see what you're going to do. So, again, it's crucial that you do exactly what you say you're going to do. Again, if you can't do it, then it's easy to just not say that you are going to do it. There is some grace for that, however, there are always things that come up. There is always a reason that a person can't go ahead and follow through with what they say, but just be careful of making excuses. Raise your standards and stop making excuses!

So many people make excuses, but they are not actually giving it their all to go ahead and follow through with what they said. So, if something does *really* come up, if something *really* has happened that you really can't get out of, then you need to let that person know ahead of time. You need to inform them, as soon as you find out that you're not going to

Persistence / Do what you Say

be able to do what you said, then you need to call that person. You need to be sending them an email. You need to be sending them a text message. Whatever you have got to do, just ensure that if you are not able to do what you said, if you are not able to keep an appointment, if you are not able to fulfil an order, whatever the case may be, if you are not able to do that, then you need to be in contact with that person. You need to let them know.

Have some respect for them and let them know the situation, because you know we all understand that things do happen, and sometimes things come up that we can't avoid, but that person's time is valuable, and you owe it to them to do what you say you're going to do.

Here's a personal example:

Addler Nicolas-My first encounter with Steven Walker was when I was doing a live video on the topic "Holding onto past pains like spoiled milk." and guess who got my attention. He jumped on and made himself known. We've been brothers ever since. Right after we set up a phone call and boy did our

Can You Hear Me Now?

past life stories come out on that phone call. No business was discussed, just past life, current life, and where we both wanted to go. We followed the same network of Danelle Delgado, Brad Lea, Grant Cardone, and Matt Manero. And then there was the 10XGrowthCon and the ticket giveaway. It seems like everyone was going for those tickets. Steven Walker said the dumbest thing ever, "I'm not going for the tickets." "I'm glad he came to his senses and went for the ticket and won. Enough people convinced me to go for the ticket. The two most influential were Steven and my wife. My first couple of videos giving the reason why I should be given the ticket. Steven called me immediately and said, "Addler at the end of it all, when your name is called will you be satisfied with your efforts?" To be totally honest I was annoyed and did not want to hear that. Steven is very good at speaking on what he knows others do not want to hear. Even though it was not what I wanted to hear, it was what I needed. My next series of videos set me apart from everyone else that was going for the tickets. It got me recognition with

Persistence / Do what you Say

Danelle Delgado and her influential circle, Ken Walls, Grant Cardone, 10X Network, and the founder of the best training platform in the entire world, Brad Lea CEO of LightSpeed VT. I won that ticket, not just from Matt Manero, but also from Brad Lea. Thank you, Steven, for pushing and coaching me to win that Golden Ticket. I remember seeing Steven in Miami thinner than I remember him from online and the face of a lion on the hunt. He was very short and clear with me that he was there for business. I said cool to catch up with you later bro. Steven was in sniper mode. He was looking for the kill. We had a chance to sit down and talk the last night of the conference. We were the last two in the lobby that night. I can't mention the 10X Growth Con without mentioning the Q&A with Grant Cardone. Steven gets up there and asks Grant "How important is it to get attention, and do I have yours?" Grant says "It's everything and yells HEEEY HEEEY. Try it. And the crowd repeats Grant Cardone and says,"Hey HEY". And Grant says, "And yes you do have my attention." Bro, it was so

Can You Hear Me Now?

freaking epic. Steven became my sponsor and helped me launch my company. I shared my business idea with Steven and even sent him a drawing I made at the 10X Growth Con. His wife created an actual mock up visual of my drawing. I will never forget that day for the rest of my life. I sent that design, 3 different designs, to my small network of close friends and my wife for them to vote. It was my dream right in front of me. I chose one and that's how the design was brought to life. I hadn't launched my business yet, but after seeing how real the design was, I could no longer hold this dream in my belly any longer. I had to give birth to it. I started advertising this design on social media many times. Detox 10X is my company and it's real. It's my dream come true.

"Humongous shout out to my sponsors at www.walkerpromotes.com. Incredible Job to my brother, great friend, mentor, and promotions manager Walker Promotes. I can't say thank you enough. Loving my charger with my personal brand Detox 10X on it. Absolutely 10X love it."

Persistence / Do what you Say

Why do people make excuses? Why don't they follow through with what they say? It seems to me that a lot of people, they don't really think too much about it. They are not purposely not doing what they say, they are just loose with their words. They will say something and they are careless with their words and it really boils down to they are selfish. They are not worried or thoughtful when it comes to other people and their time, they are not really worried about breaking an appointment or showing up late. It's just a kind of carelessness and I just don't think people are doing it on purpose to offend others. I think it's just that they are unaware. They are unaware of the problems that it may cause for some people to be constantly dealing with this issue.

For me, it causes me anxiety when I'm running late or I'm running behind for something that I said I was going to do. I will, almost every time, get hurt doing what I say I'm going to do.

Persistence

pəˈsɪst(ə)ns

noun

the fact of continuing in an opinion or course of action in spite of difficulty or opposition

Consistent

kənˈsɪst(ə)nt

adjective

acting or done in the same way over time, especially so as to be fair or accurate.

"the parents are being consistent and firm in their reactions"

Action Steps

1) Think of 5 things that you have made excuses for in the past.

    a)

    b)

    c)

    d)

    e)

2) What could you have done differently to see it through?

- 64 -

CHAPTER FIVE

Believe in Yourself

Believing in yourself. Or believing in what it is that you are doing. For a person to constantly go after something, is not an easy thing to do. They must believe in what it is they are doing. Along the way, there is going to be a lot of roadblocks and there is going to be a lot of things that are going to sway you and knock you off the planned route, of the path that you are going down. If you are not completely, absolutely sold on what it is that you are doing if you do NOT believe wholeheartedly that what you are going after is worth it, then you will have people, along with many other things, that will slow you down.

There are people who will tell you that you can't do things. The media will constantly put things in your mind to throw you off course, to keep you down, I feel that if a person does not believe in what they are doing and they do not believe in their abilities, then

Can You Hear Me Now?

they will NOT be persistent. That's what I think is the biggest setback for people who are trying to be persistent. They don't have any drive, and they are not completely sold on what it is that they are doing, so they will do things to cause themselves grief.

"If you feel like you don't deserve something, you'll do things to make sure that you never get them." - Zig Ziglar

For so long in my life, I was convinced that I wasn't worth anything. My mother told me that I wouldn't amount to anything and that I was worthless. For so many years, 29 years, I was destroying my life because I didn't believe in anything. I didn't believe in anybody else, and especially not in myself. My doubting beliefs were causing me harm. I wouldn't follow through with anything. I didn't keep a job. I didn't stay in a relationship. The only thing that I did consistently was make bad choices. Once I decided that I did have value and that I was worth something, all of that changed. Where all that changed for me was on August 19th of 2016. My wife and I were

Believe in Yourself

having some issues. I'll never forget this. It was a Friday morning. I woke up and my wife and I had been... like I said, having some struggles and just really on the edge of a divorce.

I woke up, some bags were packed for the weekend, and she had told me she was going to her mother's for the weekend. In that moment I truly believed that day that she was not coming back. She said she would be, and she did end up coming back. But in that moment, I felt like my world was coming to an end. I felt like she was not going to come back, and she was leaving me and leaving with my kids.

That Friday night, I was online and I came across Danelle Delgado. She was talking about her relationship with her significant other. Something about that, even just that title, it grabbed me. Then once I started watching the video I felt like she was talking to me. I made a connection with her automatically. I needed that connection in that moment as I was feeling alone as well as dealing with being broke and just worried about my wife, whether she was going to come back to me or not.

Can You Hear Me Now?

When she left, I had decided that I was going to use this weekend to really start working on myself and really start making changes. That's what started my whole personal development journey. That's what really got me headed on the right path. Looking back on that moment now, I am so grateful that my wife had had enough at that point. When I reached out to Danielle I didn't know if she would answer the message. I didn't know if she would even see it. I just kind of broke down and I told her everything.

I told her that I cheated on my wife. I told her all the deep, dark stuff that I normally wouldn't tell anybody. I felt like I could tell a stranger my story and that she wouldn't judge me. I am so grateful for that decision that day, because me opening and just making myself vulnerable, it opened me up to receive. I was not only able to get it off my chest but then I was able to receive the answers that she gave me.

I will never forget that moment. She told me a few truths I needed to hear in that moment. She said two things that are just key and that I will never

Believe in Yourself

forget. She said, "Steven," in regard to what my mother said, she said, "My mom said similar things and guess what, Steven? Mommy was wrong." And she said, "You are worthy." I just remember thinking, WOW, I am worthy, to me that was incredible.

Then the other thing that she said to me regarding my wife and all the mess I had created was, she just said, "You got to this point by the things that you're doing. Change those habits and change your life." To me that meant, not only did she tell me that I was worth something, but she told me how I could start amounting to something. She put that belief into my head that I was worthy and that I could accomplish things, and then she told me how to do that. I took that to heart.

I took both of those things very seriously and I felt like that was the start of the big plan for me. I was almost 29 years old and something changed in that moment. I had never truly lived. I had struggled with depression and drug addiction. I had been in and out of prison, all that bad stuff. But when she spoke those words to me, I started to believe in myself and

Can You Hear Me Now?

that is why I am so persistent. I feel like believing in yourself must be there or you will just, kind of do whatever.

You won't ever lock onto something and go for it because, if you don't believe in yourself and what you are doing, then you are just kind floating through life, useless, dreamless. If you do NOT believe in what it is that you are going after, then you are probably not going to be able to accomplish it. It's impossible to be persistent if you don't believe in yourself.

Raise your standards and stop making excuses!

Action Steps

1) What is the story that you tell yourself that holds you back?

2) What have you achieved so far and why do you deserve more?

CHAPTER SIX

Take Action

The third part of being persistent is taking action. After you have decided that it is important to do what you say and you have a strong belief in yourself, you are going to want to go after this big, scary thing that a lot of people would give up on. You must take action. Taking action is absolutely necessary if you want to be persistent.

A great example of me taking action was when I decided that I was going to lose 100 pounds. It was December 1st, 2016, I decided that I didn't want to gain any more weight. Many of my family members are overweight, this was the norm. I had got up to 300 pounds and I was feeling very unhealthy. I didn't have the energy to play with my kids. I would sleep for long hours and ultimately, I didn't feel very good about myself. So, I had to raise my standards and stop making excuses!

This was just a few months into my personal development journey, and I was starting to feel good

Can You Hear Me Now?

mentally, spiritually and emotionally, I became aware that I wasn't doing anything for my physical health. I would see people that were working out or running. I just decided one day, I was going to lose weight, and there was Alexis Paris doing a Juice to Live.

She was doing a 30-day juice challenge, it is funny to me now because it was starting on January 1st and I didn't know that. I thought it was starting on December 1st. I remember this about that moment. This was a pretty big deal to me. I think we only had $100 in our bank account and I had made the decision to go to Walmart and buy a juice machine so I could start the challenge on that day.

That was the best choice I could have made. I immediately, started what they called juicing, which is basically you grind up vegetables in a machine. It spits out the juice. Then you drink it. Even doing that taught me a lot about taking action and being persistent, because I had people all around me saying, "Hey, juicing is nasty" or "Juicing is hard." "I tried that once and I didn't like it."

Take Action

Raise your standards and stop making excuses! When I decided that I was going to lose weight, I had all sorts of outside influences telling me that what I was going after was impossible, or dumb, or not fun. It was there, all these reasons why I shouldn't succeed at it. If I wasn't being persistent, if I wouldn't have believed in myself, in what I was going after I would not have been able to follow through and take that action. I urge you to take action today!

When I could ignore that and go for it, and do the steps, every day I would wake up and I would say, "Okay, I still want to lose this weight, so these are the things that I have to do." Then the hard part is doing it. I would just push myself. After a certain period, I just naturally stopped eating the junk. I stopped drinking pop, I stopped drinking milk, I stopped eating bread. I'm down to a diet of chicken and vegetables and I've been doing that since probably January or February. That's been what I've been hungry for, and that's what I've been eating.

So, at this point, I haven't lost 100 pounds...yet! But, I have changed my life. I have changed my personal

Can You Hear Me Now?

health by taking action. I'm down, at one point I was down 85 pounds. I've kept off 80 pounds and about six sizes in my jeans. I was wearing a 2XL shirt, pushing a 3XL and now I'm wearing a 1XL and sometimes those are a little loose for me.

Taking action is absolutely necessary if you're going to be a persistent person. Taking action is probably the hardest part of being persistent. That's going back to not believing in yourself or being careless with your words. Taking action is necessary if you want to be a persistent person.

Raise your standards and stop making excuses!

What was it that gave me that drive?

Quite frankly, I just realized that I weighed 300 pounds and I didn't want to gain any more weight. I just decided that enough was enough, and I was feeling so good mentally and spiritually and things were going better with my wife, with my relationships, and I just felt like if I could be growing and learning, if I could save my marriage and if I could just start building healthier relationships then I could surely start living a healthier life.

I once heard a story told about a woodcutter and huge mighty oak tree.

The woodcutter had two options,
1. To really go for it and swing that axe so big so hard with all his might until he literally couldn't move anymore.
2. To take five strong swings at each day.

The first one would leave a few marks in the tree, but not cut it down. It would also leave the woodcutter in so exhausted and possibly injured that he would never again raise his axe.

The second option would take time, but each day it would make a good cut into that tree, until it is through enough it falls.

This is the greatest example of focused action, if each day we take a few focused action steps towards our goal, it's no longer we might reach them, it's now **when** we reach them.

Action Steps

1) Every night make a list of 5 things you will do the next day to bring you closer to your goal

2) Next day, Do the list!!!

CHAPTER SEVEN

Don't quit until the bell rings

A necessary part of being persistent is not quitting until the bell rings. Matt Manero wrote about it in his book called The Grit. Back in December, I had the great pleasure, of discovering Matt Manero. He was running what he called the 10X give-away. This was to win a ticket to Grant Cardone's 10X Growth Con. Grant Cardone did a really good job of selling this event. I was 100% convinced that I had to be at this event. I didn't know how I was going to do it, I didn't have the money to do it, I'd never been on a plane. I'd never been to Florida. I'd never been to an event like this, but I was just convinced that going to an event like this would just change everything. It would help my business, it would help my family, it would just help change my whole life.

I thank God, I discovered Matt Manero and he was running the 10X give-away. He had this contest. He said, "For those of you who want to win a ticket, I'm giving away 10 tickets, and these are the rules: you

Can You Hear Me Now?

have to do a live video and you have to submit it and you have to say why you need to be at the 10X Growth Con, where you're stuck at, and what would you do when you get back."

At the beginning, I wasn't convinced that I wanted to win the ticket. I was convinced that I would earn my ticket. So, I had a bad attitude about winning the ticket. I wanted to be the guy that earned his ticket.

I did my first couple of videos, basically just telling him that, "Hey, I want to earn my ticket." But I wasn't looking at it the right way. My perspective was off. This is where my wife stepped in and said, "Hey, Steven, if you're convinced that this is something that you need to do, if you think that going to this conference is going to change our lives, then you need to swallow your pride, you need to go for this, and you need to take it seriously." And in my mind, I was taking it seriously. I was serious about not wanting another handout.

Little did I know, that it wasn't a handout. It wasn't a giveaway. It was, you're going to work and you are going to bare your soul for this ticket. That's exactly

Don't quit until the bell rings

what I started doing. I started doing live videos. I did one video that was 20 minutes long and in that video, I shared things that I'm not happy to talk about in front of a bunch of people. I talked about being in prison. I talked about my mom abusing me. I talked about my drug usage. I talked about cheating on my wife. I mean, I talked about some stuff that I got backlash for.

I believe it was my sister that reached out to me and was basically upset about the things I said about my mom. I had my wife, when she first heard it she was a little upset that I mentioned cheating on her because it was something that embarrassed her. Yes, it was hard for me to share that story. I was so determined that going to that 10X Growth Con was going to change my life, I put everything out on the table. I decided that I wasn't going to walk away from that table or walk away from the contest not knowing that I gave it my all.

It didn't get the response I was hoping for. I thought Matt would watch that video and I would win the

Can You Hear Me Now?

ticket and then that would be the end of it. That wasn't the case.

In the second to last week, he changed the contest a little bit. He changed it so it was going to be a viewer's choice. Earlier on in the give-away, Matt and his wife had picked the winner. During this week, Matt said, "Okay, this is where I'm going to let the viewers pick. "You're going get people to like and share your video. The people that get the most likes and shares will go into the final vote. And then whoever's on the Zoom call with us will vote for the winner."

I took that video and I believed that I was going win, I knew that I was going to win, and I took action to do that. I decided that I was going to win no matter what, and so I started sending that video to people and it wasn't looking like a lot of people were supporting me. I was kind of getting to the point where I wasn't convinced that I was going to win. It was starting to get me down.

Then Matt Manero, this guy, he's just the most giving man that I know. He's not only giving away tickets,

Don't quit until the bell rings

but he's also giving of his time. His videos and posts were constantly motivating me and inspiring me to keep trying to win this ticket.

During that part of the competition, he came out with a free audio of his book. It is called The Grit. I listened to it. I have listened to it five or six times now, but the first time what I got out of it was his story about this fight that he got into. He got into this fight with a kid at school. They were at recess and he tells the story of how he was picked on as a kid. They called him Fat Matt, he was overweight. Of course, I could relate to this because I was overweight as well and I got picked on growing up.

I related to it and he talked about this one time that this sixth grader started picking on him. He said enough was enough and he fought this kid. I guess the kid was beating his butt from the very beginning all the way till the very end. The part that really stuck out to me, the part that I'll never forget, is he said,

"I fought until the bell rang."

He did not stop, the kids on the playground were begging him to stop fighting. The kid that was

Can You Hear Me Now?

beating him begged him to stop fighting, but Matt refused to quit. He refused to give up. He fought until the bell rang. Finally, the kid stopped beating him up, and that moment, that part in that book, sparked something inside of me and I decided that I wasn't going stop fighting until the bell rung. Raise your standards and stop making excuses!

I took that video, and I shared it with every single person in my inbox. I said, hey, can you like and share this? Can you join the zoom call and vote for Steven Walker because I need to win this ticket? I need to be at this 10X Growth Con. I'll do whatever it takes to get there.

I did it. There were people that whole time, that wasn't supporting me. It was very similar to the story that Matt had shared. The whole time I was fighting for my life, and I would have people come and say, "Hey, quit, give up." I had a lady from my church reach out to me and tell me that, "I was putting Grant Cardone and the 10X Growth Con before God." She said that "I was worshiping money and that I shouldn't be doing that."

Don't quit until the bell rings

That was a real slap in the face for me. Then I had people message me and tell me I'm a loser and tell me to stop spamming them." I mean I have all sorts of hate coming at me. There were very few people who said, "Hey, you're doing a great job. I want to support you. Yes, I will share it. Yes, I will like it." But I had to keep fighting. It was because of that story that Matt Manero shared that I could fight until the bell rang.

I fought until the bell rang. I stopped sending messages to my friends and family asking them to go and vote for me ten minutes before the Zoom call. I went on to that Zoom call knowing that I had done everything in my power to win that ticket, I was confident in myself that even if I didn't win, I had achieved something because I had given my all and tried my best consistently.

I will never forget that moment when the announcing of the winners started and it was obvious that I was in the final count, that I was in the vote for the win. That was SO exciting for me. I wasn't sure how many people would show up.

Can You Hear Me Now?

I will never forget. Matt Manero, when he announced it, he said, he didn't mention the winner because they were counting. He and his wife were counting. But he said, "Yeah, this looks like a landslide. He won it two to one." When he said that he won two to one, I just knew in my gut that it was me. When he said, "Steven Walker" I lost control. I started yelling and being excited. I was really fired up. It felt SO GOOD to accomplish what I set out to achieve.

Even though I was okay with not winning because I knew that I had given it my all, when I realized that I had won, it was so worth the fight. I was so glad that I didn't quit until the bell rang.

I'm so grateful that I got the opportunity from Matt Manero to win the ticket to the 10X Growth Con. I felt like before I even got to the 10X Growth Con I was a winner because I worked hard to get there, I put a lot of time and effort into winning that ticket.

I did 43 videos during that contest to win the ticket. I'm so glad that I did it that way. If I would have paid for the ticket, I wouldn't have been ready for the event. Because I did all those videos, I showed up at the Growth Con and I felt like a celebrity.

Don't quit until the bell rings

There were lots of people that came up to me and said, "Hey, you're Steven Walker, aren't you?" And I had no idea who they were. Some of the people I knew from their live videos and I felt the same way about them because it seemed liked I was seeing someone that I had seen on TV.

I could confidently look at people and talk to them, and, I had lost a bunch of weight. So, I was feeling better about myself physically. I could look people in the eye and talk to them confidently about what it is that I do. I made a lot of good connections at the 10X Growth Con.

It did so much more than what I thought it would do. I realize now, looking back, that I had no idea what one event could do to a person's life. I made new customers at that event. I met new friends. I have a couple of close friends and what I would call partners that I will be mentioning in this book. It was a great thing for me and I would recommend anybody that's thinking about going to the 10X Growth Con 2018, that they must do whatever it takes to get there.

I fought until the bell rang and so should you.

Action Steps

When you hit that wall or the end of your comfort zone, re-focus on your why.

Why are you doing this?

What are the consequences of you not achieving this?

How bad can things get if you fail at this?

Now re-think and write down your new ideas!

It is amazing what our pains can push us to.

CHAPTER EIGHT

Care about people

After you've mastered being persistent and you know what that's all about, and you've decided that you're going to be a persistent person, I want you to consider another concept. And this is the concept of gifting. Giving gifts to prospects, family members, any person that you are wanting to get attention from, gifting is a very effective way to do so.

The first thing that you must do to start considering gifting is you must care about people. So that's just the basics of giving a gift to someone. The reason that I started thinking about gifting is that of something Zig Ziglar said.

"You can have anything you want in life if you'll just help enough people get what they want."

Can You Hear Me Now?

If it is more customers that you want, if it is happier employees that you want, if it is more loyal customers that you are looking for, you must care about what they want. You must find a way to give them something that says you care about them, and I found that gifts are a very good way to show people that you care about them, if done properly.

I think a lot of people do give gifts. The problem is, they are giving the gift for selfish reasons. They're maybe giving a gift they would like to receive or something they want to show off, instead of finding out what it is the person is into or needs. The people I have gifted to others would state they are out of my league. What gift do you give to a millionaire or a billionaire? I'm obviously not able to afford the things that he/she can afford so if I find that the person I am buying for likes cigars, I'm not going to buy him a cigar and send it to him. First, it's something that he's going to smoke and forget about, second, he can afford the most expensive cigars and I can't. It makes sense to me, not to send him a cigar but to find something that is still valuable to him. Maybe something he has overlooked that could really

Care about people

help him. So, there are three key things you need to know if you're going to start gift giving. The first thing that
you must consider when giving a gift is that you must consider the person that you are giving it to.
In my industry, so many businesses consider a gift as something that has their name on it. When really, that's not a gift. That's more of a promotional product. That's something that's going to generate revenue for your business and most of the time other people don't consider that a gift. It ends up going to Goodwill, it ends up in the trash or set aside, because they feel like they are advertising for someone else.
You must care about the person that you're giving the gift to. That's not negotiable. If you don't care about the person, don't even bother giving them a gift because it's probably something that isn't received the way that you want it to be and that defeats the whole purpose of giving the gift.
A great example of caring about someone that you're giving a gift to is something that I found when I first started my business, Walker Promotes. I found that

Can You Hear Me Now?

my problem was I did not know enough people, and enough people don't know who I am, so it was my duty, it's my obligation to make sure that people know who I am. Not only do they know who I am, but they like me and they want to buy from me and to ensure that they don't forget my. That's why my motto with Walker Promotes is *"Never Forget a Customer, Never Let a Customer Forget You."* In the very beginning of my journey I stumbled across this by accidence, I went searching online and there was a hat company offering samples, I decided that the best way was to send them a logo and they put that business logo on a hat. Then they sent it to me for free. I then took it to my prospects, and they really appreciated that.

That's the idea that was sold to me, and I thought it was just crazy enough to work. I started calling on these businesses. For several months I would call businesses and nobody would really pay attention to me. Nobody would act like they were going to give me any time because I wasn't providing value to them, I was simply going in there and saying, "Hey,

Care about people

I want to sell you something." And nobody's got time for that. Nobody's interested in that.

It wasn't until I started showing people that I cared about them that I was able to start getting my foot into some of these doors. What I would do, once I realized that I could produce hats. I did go into businesses that would tend to ignore me, and then suddenly, the gate keeper or secretary would allow me to talk to the owner. They would then give me the right to spend some time with the person that made the decision.

By me showing people that hey, this guy doesn't do promotional products like the other companies, I was able to go over there and sell my products to them. I started earning their business just by showing them that I cared about them.

A perfect example of giving a gift to somebody and not caring about that person is my very own example. I was really excited about creating Walker Promotes, so what I did is I had my wife design some t-shirts and we bought two dozen t-shirts to send out to people. They were not well received at all. There

Can You Hear Me Now?

were people that said, "Thank you" but I felt like they were saying thank you out of obligation, not because they appreciated the shirt. Since then, I have not seen anyone wearing those shirts.
I literally just threw that money away. I spent a couple hundred bucks and I didn't get anything in return and so it would have been better if I would have given them nothing.

*"Never Forget a Customer,
Never Let a Customer
Forget You."*

Action Steps

1) Think of your best customer experience, what happened, how did it make you feel?

2) Think of the last time a friend or family member made you feel great, what happened, how did it make you feel?

"If you push for sales, you will get some sales, if you build relationships, you will have a life time customer that will buy again and again."

CHAPTER NINE

Be willing to give

The next part of giving gifts is that you must be willing to give. Once you've decided that you care about people, and you know the right type of gifts to give, then you must be willing to give.

I have found that it's very easy to make excuses and reasons why you shouldn't give. I am always looking for excuses to go ahead and give. I'd love to give you an example of this, the Real Brad Lea, owner of LightSpeed VT.

We were down to I believe it was $131 in our account and we spent $100 of it to buy a pair of headphones, the Rhapsody headphones with the Lightspeed VT logo on them, and then we also got a Ten Four battery pack with a picture of Brad Lea the Bottom Line on it, because that's something that's personal to him.

We were caring about Brad Lea. We didn't send him gifts that said Walker Promotes on it because he doesn't want to promote us. At this point when we sent the gifts to Brad Lea, he knew who I was, but he

Can You Hear Me Now?

had never said my name, he had never acknowledged me. You know, I think he'd probably seen some of my videos trying to win the 10X Growth Con ticket. But he never paid me any attention.

I decided that I was going to put it all out there. I talked my wife into spending that $100 when I only had $131. I spent that $100 because I did not want to settle for not getting his attention. I wanted to be heard by Brad. So, I did it. I took that chance. I have never looked back from that and I'll always remember the acknowledgment that I received from sending him those gifts.

Brad Lea did a 12-minute Facebook Live video where he talked about me and me only and you can find that on my website or you can also find that on YouTube.

youtube/c/stevenwalkerpromotes

Brad Lea generates millions of dollars in revenue every year. They call him the Real Brad Lea because he always keeps it real. He doesn't say things just to make you feel good. He tells it how he sees it. He's a great guy, he just doesn't worry about hurting

Be willing to give

people's feelings. If you ask him a question, you better be ready for an answer. He's not going sugar coat it. He's just going tell you what he thinks.

That is why I ultimately wanted to reach out to him and connect with him. I like the guy. I really respect him. Not only as a businessman but as a father and as a man in general. I really do have a lot of respect for him.

So, I decided that I wanted to do business with Brad Lea. I decided to raise my standard, I decided that he was going hear me and I wasn't going to stop until he did hear me.

Action Steps

This step will help your mindset.

The challenge is to give your time, money **or** a gift.

To a loved one, a stranger **and** yourself.

CHAPTER TEN

Do not tolerate being unheard.

The next part and the most important part of gift giving. If you've decided that you care about people, and you've gotten to the point where you're willing to give, you must come to a point where you will not tolerate being unheard. Raise your standards and stop making excuses!

You must demand the attention, you must what my good friend Grant Cardone says, *"You have to do whatever it takes to be heard."* If you've decided that you want to get someone's attention, if you consider someone a target like I did with Brad Lea, you cannot tolerate anything less than being heard.

To paint a picture of why it's so important to do that, I would like to share with you what happened after I sent these gifts to Brad Lea. After he did the live video promoting me in a huge way. I gained more customers, I gained a lot of confidence, people took me more seriously after they had watched this

Can You Hear Me Now?

video, and not only that, Brad became one of my customers.

After I met him at the 10X Growth Con I got a few minutes of his time. We got to shake hands. We got to connect on a personal level, then shortly after the 10X Growth Con, April 26th was the date, he made a purchase from me that was the same amount as my income the year before. So, just in that one order, from this one relationship, I could lock in with gifting, I got one year's worth of income. Not only that, now, he's my customer. Again, I take you back to my motto because now, it's my duty and my obligation to make sure that *"I never forget a customer and that he never forgets me."* I'll never let Brad Lea forget me.

That's the type of attitude that I have when I'm going after these prospects and these future customers. I never want them to forget about me, and I'll never forget them. That is where I've used my persistence to push that relationship along. Whatever it was that I was lacking like with Brad we tried messaging him

Do not tolerate being unheard.

a lot. This was not getting the job done? Calling his office wasn't getting the job done.

The next step for me, after I had exhausted myself when I was ready to give up, I decided to send him a gift. I am so glad that I did that. Best decision ever! I'm so glad that I did not tolerate being unheard. As Brad Lea hearing me was a big part of my journey into getting another people's attention. The way Brad Lea responded to me when I sent him these gifts is probably the biggest reason that I'm writing this book now.

Once he had responded to me in such a positive way, so grateful for not only the gifts but the time, money and thought that had gone into these gifts, I found that I could influence people with not only my persistence but with gift-giving. I decided to turn it up a notch. I decided to start giving on a higher level. I started giving more to people of even bigger influence. All in all, I probably only spent $2000. But with that $2000 I could get a lot of attention from a lot of different people. They were received so well, so appreciative, sharing their

Can You Hear Me Now?

gratitude with their audiences, gaining a lot more customers, connections, and new relationships.

Never give up! Failure and rejection are only the first step to succeeding.

Action Steps

1) Think of 5 people / clients that have said no recently.

    a)
    b)
    c)
    d)
    e)

2) Pick 3 serve them, instead of selling to them.

3) Follow up with them and write your results.

CHAPTER ELEVEN

Be willing to hear NO

Another important part of being persistent is knowing that people are going to tell you NO. You will hear this a lot more often than you will hear yes. Getting good at hearing NO is not only big in persistence, but it's big in life, it's big in sales, it's big in this world. If you think of a small child, I've got four small children, and they love cookies, but like most children, they always want more, but this is not good for them, so we must tell them NO, again and again. This doesn't mean we don't love them, or like them, it doesn't mean we think they are unworthy of the cookies, it's not a bad thing! We need to change our perspective on how we react to the word NO, some say NO stands for Next Opportunity, or the beginning of NOt yet!

No is a part of life. No is something that we're going to hear over and over. Daily, we going to hear no's whether it's from our wife, our kids, from our

Can You Hear Me Now?

employers, from our customers or prospective customers, or business partners. Learning to not hear NO in a negative way is a big part of getting another people's attention.

It is as important as being persistent because without persistence a person will just give up, especially if they are in sales. It is hard to hear the word no. When the bills are past-due and you are stressing out about that, it is hard not to make the sale. It is hard when you spend a lot of time with somebody and you still hear that word no at the end.

What I have found is that it is important that you are willing to hear that no, and that you do not take it personally. Like my example with my children. You hear the no, you let that feeling go and then you go find out why they are saying no. Are they saying no because they do not like you? Are they saying no because they do not believe in your product or service? Are they saying no because they simply have no need for what you must offer? What is the reason behind the no? why they are saying no? If you can find out the reason, this gives you something

Be willing to hear NO

to work on or improve, and if it is simply that they do not have the need then this is a great opportunity to get referrals from them for others that will need your product or services.

Another thing I found that has been very helpful in the process of learning to be more willing to hear the no, is to realize that it is not all about me. The person may not be saying no to me. They might be saying no because their wife discouraged them against the purchase. They might be saying no because of an experience, or maybe I am not giving them all the information they require. Maybe they don't understand the information.

There are lots and lots of reasons that a person would say no. So again, do not take it personally and be willing to hear the word no.

Another important note here, is to not treat your customers or prospects like a pay check, if you have that needy desperation about you, because you are behind on your bills etc. This will show, they will feel this in the way that you speak to them, in the way that you react to their response. You need to stop

Can You Hear Me Now?

seeing them as $$$'s and focus on their needs and how you can really help them.

Action Steps

1) Think of the last 3 things that you said NO to.

   a)
   b)
   c)

2) Now write the reasons why you said NO

   a)
   b)
   c)

3) Reflect on these answers and see how these shift your beliefs on why people say NO to you,

CHAPTER TWELVE

Having the right attitude

We have decided that we care about people, we have become willing to give, and we have decided that we are going to give, also we are not going to tolerate being unheard. Then something kind of funny happens. It's like a test, you send out this gift and you don't hear anything in response. You don't hear a thank you. For me, let's just say I sent out 10 packages. And I spend quite a bit of money on that. That was the little bit of money that I had left. And I was doing that to grow my business. I was doing that to get these people's attention, and I was expecting something out of it. I wanted to hear a thank you. I wanted to get an order out of it. There was a lot riding on this gift.

Something I have discovered is how everyone is so different; some people are not as quick to say thank you for a gift. I am quick to say thank you for a gift. Since gifting I have learned that I had to be patient as well as persistent, not only to get that person's

Can You Hear Me Now?

attention, but to get a thank you, or even to find out whether the person received the gift or not. I have a perfect example for this.

Most of you know super coach Michael Burt. This guy is incredible. I've learned so much about being a better person in general because of super coach Michael Burt. He talks about the million dollars follow up, and it's really helped me out a lot.

I decided that I wanted to send him a gift, I sent the gift back in June, maybe it was July. I tracked the parcel, so I could check and follow up, as soon as I knew that it had arrived. I received a notification saying that it had arrived. My process is, once I see that the parcel has arrived, I will message the person and I will say, "Hey, my gift has arrived. Please let me know your thoughts and feed about the products." Nine times out of ten the person will say, "Yes, I got it. I will get back to you soon, to let you know what my thoughts." Well, for whatever reason, Coach Burt did not get it. It didn't arrive. He is a busy guy. He is always on the road. He talks to realtors. He talks

Having the right attitude

to all sorts of different businessmen. He has many speaking engagements and is always on the road on the road. He has partnered up with Grant Cardone. He really is all over the place.

This caused it to take a while for him to receive the gift. It was sitting in the mail room at his office, and a month had passed by and he still hadn't received it. This whole process was like a lesson to be learned, a person can take that one of two ways. I looked at it as another opportunity to show super coach Michael Burt how persistent I am. I know others may have had a bad attitude about this situation. I've actually met myself in the past thinking, "Oh Man, this person doesn't appreciate my gifts. I spent the money and I took the time. I sent this extra special gift for this person and they are not showing the proper appreciation. They are not saying thank you, they are not returning my messages, they are ignoring me." They are not meeting my expectations. This was a great lesson for me and allowed me to use the tools and strategies I had recently learned in my personal development journey. This allowed me to step up,

Can You Hear Me Now?

raise my standards, and stop making excuses. I realized in this situation it is VERY important to have a great attitude, and show how great a person you are, because if you have a bad attitude, or if you are unkind or unprofessional then they have a good excuse for writing you off completely. That would be a great shame and a wasted opportunity, that you cannot buy back.

See, the truth is that people don't care about me and what I have got going on, they don't have the time to care, they have their own things going on and they care about what it is going on in their life and what is important to them. You still can't expect everyone to be as excited about what you are doing as you are. The key here is, you need to stay focused throughout this whole process and you need to keep a great attitude.

So, to make this point clear, I will tell you, that if you do send a gift to somebody, and you don't get the response that you were hoping for, make sure that you keep a good attitude because the second that you

Having the right attitude

lose your cool, the second that you have a bad attitude with this prospect, customer, employee, or whoever it is that you are giving the gift to, whether it is your wife or your kids, if you act upset with them, or you have a bad attitude because you're not getting the response you were hoping for, because they aren't meeting your expectations, then you just wasted a gift, my friend. So again, make sure that you have a good attitude when you are giving gifts.

Attitude is a little thing that makes a big difference.

Winston Churchill

Action Steps

1) Think of 3 times you responded badly.

    a)

    b)

    c)

2) How could you have changed that situation / responded differently.

FINAL CHAPTER

How I Can Help You

"Are any of your prospects ignoring you? Are they *all* answering your phone calls? Are they all answering your emails?" Many would say that somebody in their life is ignoring them. What I have done in this moment when I am being ignored, I will take a little bit of money out of my pocket, time and effort to create it, and I will get a gift that's personal to the person that is ignoring me. I will send it to them. Then almost immediately the person will reach back out to me and say, "Hey, I've just been busy. ......" Then, BOOM. "Thank you for the gift. Now, what do you have in mind? How can I help you?" A gift gives me the opportunity to share with them what I can do for them because again, if they don't know who you are, they cannot help you and you cannot help them. They must know you,

Can You Hear Me Now?

trust you, and like you. I found that giving gifts is a good way to get to know people. When you are following up with prospects always be persistent, it is absolutely necessary. When you're trying to show your employees that you care about them or you are wanting to keep loyal customers it is necessary. I will share with you what I have been able to do with limited resources and limited skills. So, if you are reading this right now and you are a company owner that, for example, is bringing in two million a year, you have excellent sales skills and you have an unlimited amount of resources, I can help you make even more of an impact with those resources and skills. I can help you by simply going after those people that are ignoring you. First, I would have you comprise a list of 10 customers that would really increase your business. If they knew who you were, what if they would answer your phone calls if they would give you that appointment, and if they would entertain the thought of talking to you about what it is that you can do for them. This would also get you more referrals. This will help you to make more

How I Can Help You

friends and it helps you add $$$'s 000's to the bottom line of your business. So, when you are trying to grow your business, you are looking for fresh referrals, you want to tell your employees that you appreciate them and you want to keep loyal customers. It is important to focus on them, and not to get stuck thinking about yourself, and your own issues, think more about the person that you are going to connect with. Think about your prospects, think about your employees, think about your existing customers. We will focus on these top 10 prospects that you have, we will focus on what it is that they do. Think about what they are passionate about and then together we are going to put together a plan to send them incredible and thoughtful gifts. This is going to work wonders for you. I know it sounds like a simple process. It sounds like it is something that it is too simple to work, but I have proven it for myself time and time again and I have many examples of how this has worked for me, I would like to share this one example of a time that this worked.

Can You Hear Me Now?

At the VIP Dinner with Danielle Delgado at the #10XGrowthCon 2017, I met Steven Walker of Walker Promotes. He was full of energy and ready to take his life and career to the next level. In fact, that night...he came prepared with "products" to share. After the event ended, I received a message from Steven ...he was confident and energetic...ready to set the world on fire with his "ideas", "products', and services. That was the day, I purchased my "personalized" battery pack Steven was persistent & consistent with his message. We continued to speak over the next few months when he announced his trip to Vegas to see #TheRealBradLea at that time, I told him I was going to Dallas to attend the 20th Year Anniversary Convention of Youngevity. Without hesitation, Steven recommended I go to meet Mr. Matt Manero ...known among us #10Xer's as the man with true "GRIT" ...the next "100 Million Dollar Man". I told Steven, that I didn't want to go empty handed... so, together we came up with ideas for "gifts" for Mr. Manero. I decided that whether Mr. Manero was available or not ...I would drop off these gifts provided by Walker Promotes. As expected, Steven's energy was off the charts and he couldn't wait to until I delivered the "goods". Of course, "Mr. Manero" had no 'white spaces" left on his daily schedule. However, as Danelle Delgado teaches...influence matters and Steven's influence was what we needed to get our meeting with President and CEO of CFF, Mr. Matt Manero. The day finally was here...My friend Cathy & I went to visit ..."Mr. Manero" at the CFF offices in Carrollton TX...the energy of the building was positive and on purpose. The reception was welcoming. It was such a rewarding experience, and the response on Mr. Manero's face was "priceless" after receiving the gifts. I sincerely thank Mr. Manero for his time, and generous welcoming spirit. The experience was definitely #10X and one we will never forget how it made us feel to share Steven's vision on gift giving.

Sincerely, Tina Williams

About the Author

Steven Walker is the CEO of Walker Promotes. He lives with his wife Cassie and 4 kids (Noah, Rosalie, Elijah, and Delaney) in El Dorado, Kansas. Steven's childhood was difficult, to say the least. He has overcome neglect and abuse mentally and physically as a child, foster care as a teen, and prison as a young adult. His childhood has prepared him to write "Can You Hear Me Now?". Since being ignored as a child he has mastered the art of pushing through the noise and being persistent to get his message to across and is passionate about helping others to be heard. He has been able to get the attention of Brad Lea, Grant & Elena Cardone, John Hamlin, Rocco Jackintelle and Maci Bookout & Farrah Abraham from MTV's hit tv show Teen Mom.
www.walkerpromotes.com

Thank you

Jake Duerksen

The first time I had the chance to get to know Jake, I was doing Scrap Metal Recycling. I had just taken a job to cut up some huge boilers at an old hospital in Newton Kansas. Going into the job I thought I would make plenty, to pay Jake and I both but that's not what happened! I found out in the first day that we didn't have the equipment to move enough of the metal to make any money. This is when I realized what type of person Jake is. I made it pretty clear that I didn't know how much I would be able to pay him if anything and he continued to go help me for 4 whole days. Jake is a hard worker and that's putting it lightly. What I like most about Jake is that he's always willing to help. The day after I decided I would write this book I decided I needed some pictures taken. I called two "professional photographers" in town to get a quote and neither one of them bothered to call me back until after the job was done. I called Jake up and he said he could do it the next day and guess what! He did what he said. Jake is always willing to help someone and most importantly if he says he's going to do something he does it. Jake is a big part of what motivates me to keep pushing because I want to build something so big that I can help him live the life he dreams of. Jake is not only a buddy of mine but more like a brother.
Let's go fishing soon Jake.

Dave Callaway

The first mentor that I had who really gave me his time is Dave Callaway. Dave ran a very successful insurance business here in El Dorado Kansas. When I say successful I mean ten years after they closed the doors people in town are still talking about the service that they couldn't find anywhere else. In the few years that I've known Dave, he has given me a lot of nuggets of wisdom. One day I was getting ready for a meeting with a well-known millionaire in Kansas. I expressed to Dave that I was feeling a little nervous. I did not know that the words that he said on that day would change my life in such a huge way. He said, "Walker he puts his pants on the same way you do." I went into the meeting with more confidence than I thought possible because I remembered those words from Dave. At that meeting this guy told me to look outside of El Dorado, to think bigger. Two days later I drove to Denver Colorado to meet some very successful strangers and then 4 days after that my wife and I started Walker Promotes. I truly do not know where I would be or what I would be doing if Dave hadn't told me those simple words of encouragement that day. Dave, I want to thank you here for all the wisdom you have shared with me. Being able to learn about business from you is something I believe most are missing. I will always be grateful for the time I have had with you. You've been a great friend and mentor to me. My family and I appreciate your involvement in our success.
Your Friend, Walker Texas Ranger

Melvin Walker

My dad has always been my hero. My mom and dad split up when I was too young to remember. When I lived with my mom, her and my step dad were abusive to me mentally and physically. I was an awkward little boy getting picked on constantly at school. The kids didn't know what I dealt with at home. Then I would go home and it was even worse. The bullying was there all day every day. The only time I got away from this environment was when I went with my Dad. My mom had full custody of us kids and my dad had visits with us every other week. These visits were a relief for me. I loved going to be with my dad and even his wife that I didn't care for at the time was nicer to me than my mom. Sometimes my dad would have to work and miss trips but other times that I remember much more clearly. He would drive 3.5 hours to come visit us and if he was five minutes late my mom would not let him see us. I hated my mom for that. I hated it when I couldn't go with my dad. We didn't have the most time together but when we were together he always taught me things. He would have great talks with me and make me feel loved. My dad is a huge part of this wanting to be heard. My mom didn't give me a voice at all but when I was with my dad he gave me attention that I was starving for. The more he gave me the more I wanted and I've seen this carry over into my personal relationships and in my business. I have an insatiable hunger to be heard. And I wouldn't have named this book Can You Hear Me Now if it

wasn't for my dad's involvement. I wouldn't have known that it felt so good to be heard if it wasn't for the attention he gave me. My dad has always been very supportive of our business and I can say if it wasn't for him Walker Promotes wouldn't be as successful as it has been. Thank you, Dad, for being a light in such a dark place. I know without a doubt that you've always loved me and wanted the best for me.
I love you and appreciate everything.
Sincerely, Your Son

Sherry Gillihan

I would like to say thank you to Sherry my wife's mom. She owns a company called Sign Solutions. Before I started Walker Promotes I was working hourly installing Guttering and I was also getting paid commission for selling the guttering. It wasn't going the way I had hoped and I didn't always see eye to eye with my boss. One day I was visiting with Sherry and she mentioned maybe I could sell promotional products for her. I immediately liked the idea and started doing it along with the guttering. It wasn't long after that that the boss no longer needed me around. I started working full time for Sherry. Just like with any business I had differences in opinion with Sherry. I was a lot of times very open about these differences and on some occasions, I wasn't the easiest to deal with. Sherry was always very patient with me and tried her best to make things work. Sherry I really appreciate the opportunity you gave Cassie and I to not only learn a new industry but to now own our own business. Thank you for giving us a chance and for being so patient with me especially.
Sincerely Steven

Addler Nicolas

I first came across Addler Nicolas on his Facebook Live Video. The title was "crying over spilled milk" or something along those lines. I immediately got on the phone with him after the video and we hit it off right away. I was dealing with some minor issues in my life and his problems made mine look small in comparison. The thing about that though is that even with his situation looking a lot worse, he had a better attitude. Since we met through Facebook, we spoke on the phone on a regular basis. He has been a great friend and mentors to me. Addler has a few of things that he does and he does them very well. For one he's a man of God. Second, he is a husband. Third, he is a father to 7 children. He handles these roles extremely well. Addler has a ton on his plate but you wouldn't ever know it by the way he acts. Calm cool and collected. Addler Inspires me each day. He sings beautiful music. Check his music out on YouTube. He is An Inspirational Speaker. Addler is way above average and it's exciting to watch him Excel at the rate he has. Addler thank you, brother, for always a friend and mentor to me. I am proud to know you and you'll always have a place in my Heart. Your Brother, Steven

Tina Williams

I first met Tina at the #10xgrowthcon. I had seen her in a few different FB Lives but I had also messaged her occasionally. Tina was very friendly and the moment we met, we spoke together for a good couple of hours at Danelle Delgado's VIP dinner. It was a great way for calm down, and relax a bit. I was previously so nervous and anxious, as I had never flown, been to Florida or to a big event like that and I was able to express that to her. We became friends right away. We got a hold of each other after the Conference and she ordered a Battery pack from me for her personal business Now Wellness. Tina really cares about the well-being of others. She is giving people the opportunity to live a healthier lifestyle using supplements and essential oils. I have used both of her products and I am impressed with the quality. I am also impressed with Tina's knowledge about the products and what is good for each person's different needs. I recently did a health evaluation with her and I was able to see some of the problems I am having. With Tina's help, I am now starting to take better care of myself at a young age. Tina is not only helping me with my health but she is also a good form of support. I am able to share struggles or successes with her. She always listens well and then offers her thoughts. It is tough to find a friend like this and I am very grateful that we crossed paths.
Tina thank you for being a customer of mine, but more than that thank you for being a friend to me.
I really appreciate you.
Your Friend, Steven

Forever Family Forever Free

I first met Laura Helen about a year ago. We met on Facebook. We became friends quickly. She shared her daughter's (Tegan Helen) story with me and sent me copies of her books so that I could read them. I thoroughly enjoyed the books and was happy to promote this family wherever possible.

In doing this I could help them get one book deal and it went extremely well for Matthew Cybulski. Matthew's book "Find Your Playlist" went straight up to Amazon #1 Best Seller and an International Best Seller.

I was very excited to finally write my first book! Laura and her husband David are doing an incredible job publishing people's stories. They made this whole process very easy for me. I could just tell them the stories I wanted to share in this book and they typed it all up and created a book. I was especially impressed that they didn't change up a bunch of the words. They kept it true to me, the way I said it, which is the way I wanted it done.

I would recommend Forever Family Forever Free to anyone who is looking to create and publish a book! They will help you put your story on paper very quickly and efficiently.
Thank you Forever Family Forever Free
for making my dream of being a Amazon
Best Selling Author becomes a reality.
Sincerely, Steven

Dedication

I've decided to dedicate this first book to my oldest Son Noah Eugene Walker who is 5 years old. He has always shown a lot of interest in what I do. Noah, it is with great pride that I wrote this book and it makes me even more proud to have you as a son. I'm so happy that you want to follow in my footsteps. I will make sure to keep reaching higher for our family so you'll naturally follow my lead. I love you, Noah. Noah has his own business called Noah Promotes. He even does Live Videos on Facebook once a week.
Go check him out!
   https://facebook.com/NoahPromotes

Walkerpromotes.com
**Book Me to speak at your next event
or Training Seminar**

Book me to speak at your event and I will guarantee to deliver an incredibly **INSPIRING**,
highly **ENTERTAINING** and truly **BUSINESS FOCUSED** experience for everyone in attendance.
My unique style combines, creating a Persistent mindset with my unbelievable true stories,
keeping them engaged with my high energy delivery,
And **EMPOWERING** them with actionable strategies to take their **RESULTS** to the next level.

My topics are,

- Persistence
- The power of gift giving
- How to communicate more effectively.
- Having the right attitude
- How to create relationships with winners.
- How to become unstoppable and powerful!

Would you like me to create some persistence, resistance, and strategies to create winners at your next event?

Whether you would like to book a workshop a talk, or a bulk order of books, please use the contact details below to get in touch.

Steven@walkerpromotes.com
CALL- 316-251-1220

I look forward to connecting with you.

Walker Promotes is very excited to Promote your business any way we can! We provide promotional items such as apparel (t-shirts, hats, etc), pens, golf balls, and many other promotional items.

For all your Promotional needs
facebook.com/promotionalservices1234
Steven@walkerpromotes.com
CALL- 316-251-1220

See all gift ideas at
walkerpromotes.com/store

Thank you

Rondi & Michelle Lambeth
Addler Nicolas
Laura Helen
Tina Williams
Dianne Bushelle-Belgrave
Ryan Williams
Matthew Cybulski
Luis Guevara
Gary Pollard
Brenda Phillips
Joshua Lattieri
Rodney Martin Waits
Jake Duerksen
Michael Burt
Sarah Williams
Nicole Zeien-Cox
Stephen Fitch
Kyle Hendrix
Anthony Santangelo
Elton Sherwood
Shane Ray

Make a commitment today!

What 5 steps do you need to complete?

Never Give Up!

www.ingramcontent.com/pod-product-compliance
Lightning Source LLC
Chambersburg PA
CBHW070246230526
45470CB00002B/489